NATURE NOTES

THE NEW COLLECTION

NATURE NOTES

THE NEW COLLECTION

Peter Brookes

LITTLE, BROWN AND COMPANY

A *Little, Brown* Book

These 'Nature Notes' cartoons first published in *The Times* between July 1997 and June 1999
First published in this collection in Great Britain in 1999 by Little, Brown and Company

ISBN: 0 316 64856 6

Typeset by M Rules in Bembo
Printed and bound in Great Britain by Butler & Tanner Ltd, Frome and London

Little, Brown and Company (UK)
Brettenham House
Lancaster Place
London WC2E 7EN

For Angela, Benjamin and William

Neil Hamilton, the publicity-seeking former MP for Tatton, is severely censured by the Downey Report on the cash-for-questions scandal.

NATURE NOTES

Fig. 1 Lying toad

Giant Toad (*Hamiltonus corruptus*)

A species once protected by the authorities, this clammy creature crawls out from under stones to seek exposure. The female is dominant.

In Northern Ireland nationalist violence erupts when the RUC allows the most contentious Orange parade of the season down the Catholic Garvaghy Road from Drumcree.

NATURE NOTES

Two Weevils

The *genus* causes enormous damage to the fabric of society. It thrives in a climate of high temperature, on rare occasions proving responsive to pest control.

Fig. 1 Greater Weevil
(*Ira nationalista*)

Fig. 2 The Lesser of Two Weevils
(*Orangeus rerouteus*)

The parliamentary hot-house nurtures a number of ripely flavoured nutcases.

Sinn Féin states that it would accept an interim peace accord that falls well short of the united Ireland for which the IRA has fought for decades.

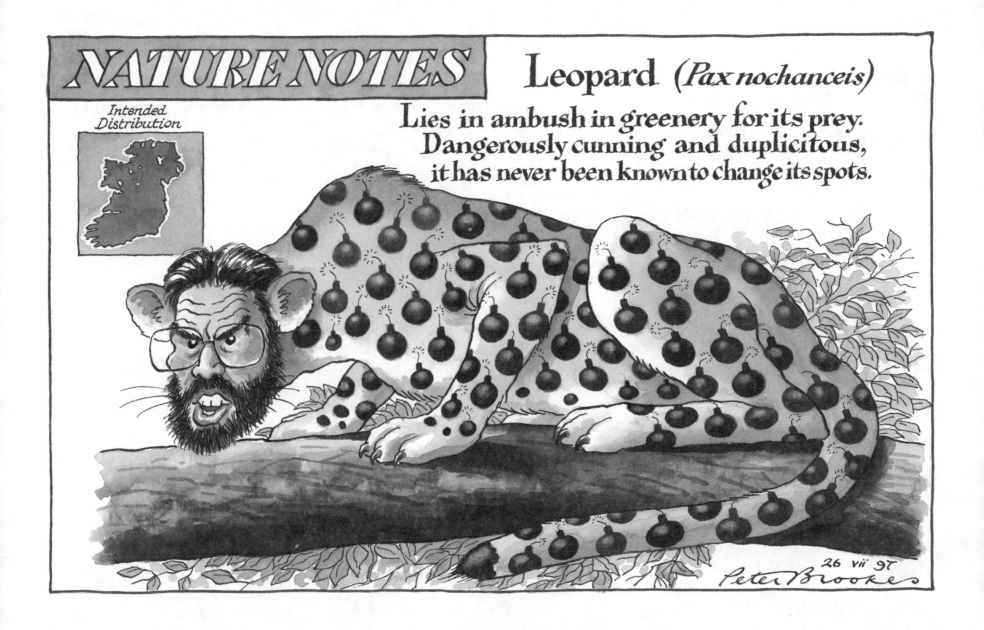

NATURE NOTES

Leopard (*Pax nochanceis*)

Lies in ambush in greenery for its prey.
Dangerously cunning and duplicitous,
it has never been known to change its spots.

Intended
Distribution

26 vii 97

Peter Brookes

While the Prime Minister holidays in Tuscany, his famously prickly deputy, John Prescott, holds the fort with a meddling Minister Without Portfolio, Peter Mandelson. A competitive game, for two players.

Scots vote overwhelmingly in a devolution referendum for a Scottish parliament with tax-varying powers ('Yes–Yes'). The SNP leader Alex Salmond sees this as a first step towards independence.

NATURE NOTES

Fig.1 Serving suggestion

SALT

THE SCOTSMAN

It is hard to swallow,
so take with a large
pinch of salt.

Scotch Salmond
(Fullindependencis orbustus)
The height to which it can leap
is probably exaggerated as it
navigates a slippery slope.
Extremely fishy and oily.

Peter Brookes
13 ix 97

Lord Tebbit, speaking at a Tory conference fringe meeting in Blackpool, revisits his infamous cricket-test analogy by stating that multiculturalism is a divisive force. New Tory leader William Hague slaps him down.

NATURE NOTES

Blue-footed Booby
(*Tebbitus crickettestus*)

This seabird can plunge from a great height into the shallows *(see Fig.1)*. Of a hostile and insular disposition, it tends to attack immigratory species.

Fig.1 The booby heads for extinction.

Peter Brookes 11 x 97

The Queen's state visit to India is marred by a storm over Foreign Secretary Robin Cook's private offer to help find a 'just solution' to the dispute over Jammu and Kashmir.

NATURE NOTES

Cock Robin
(Sanctimonious foreignsecretarius)

More comfortable at home in its natural habitat, it will noticeably wilt when the heat is on. Stroppy little breeder in territorial disputes. Polygamous.

Fig. 1 Putting its foot in it

Christine Hamilton is involved in a bizarre press conference in Westminster to refute the 'sleaze' charges brought against her husband. Tony Blair rules out allowing government time for an anti-foxhunting Bill.

NATURE NOTES

Vixen *(Hamiltona brownenvelopa)*

Fiercely protective of her charge when pursued by newshounds. Devious and cunning in her futile rebuttal of the classification as vermin.

Fig: 1

The new public standards watchdog advises the Labour Party to return a £1 million donation from the head of Formula One motor-racing, Bernie Ecclestone. The sport is subsequently exempted by the government from a tobacco sponsorship ban aimed at ending cigarette advertising.

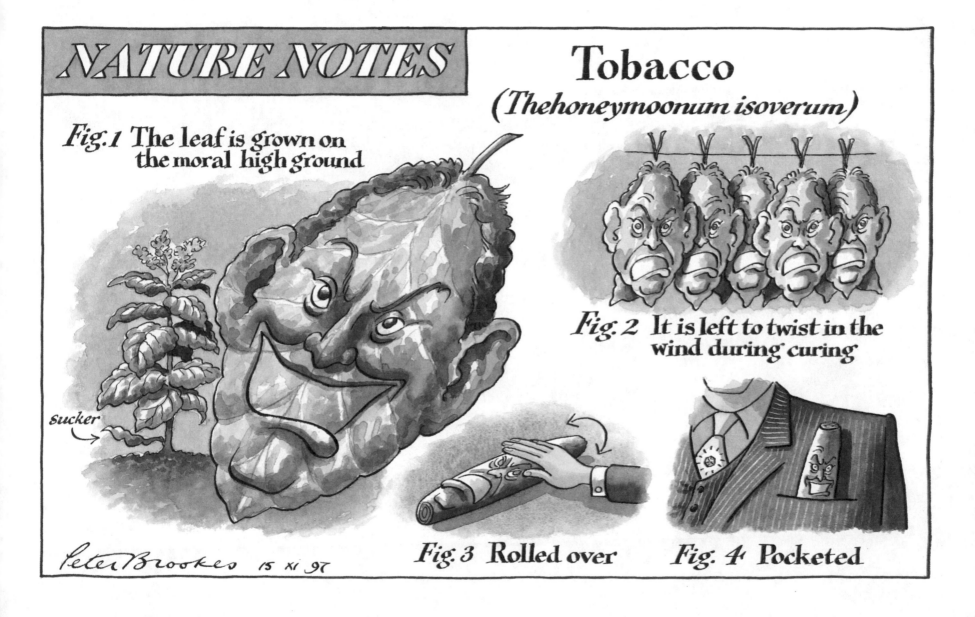

NATURE NOTES

Tobacco
(Thehoneymoonum isoverum)

Fig.1 The leaf is grown on the moral high ground

sucker

Fig.2 It is left to twist in the wind during curing

Fig.3 Rolled over

Fig.4 Pocketed

Peter Brookes 15 xi 97

Geoffrey Robinson, Paymaster General, is revealed to be the beneficiary of a Guernsey offshore trust (set up for him by the mysterious Mme Bourgeois) just as he is preparing to announce that the government's new and widely criticised savings scheme would deprive thousands of savers of their tax benefits.

NATURE NOTES

keep well-trust

Fig.1 In deep doo-doo

Robinson's Guernsey Tomato (*Youmustus trustus*)

This 'Money-maker' variety, when introduced to the hot-house atmosphere of Westminster, can produce red faces all round. For bourgeois tastes.

13 Xii 97
Peter Brookes

Home Secretary Jack Straw, having unveiled a series of initiatives tackling youth crime and preached the importance of parental responsibility, is embarrassed by his son being accused of dealing in cannabis.

President Bill Clinton could face impeachment and five years in jail if he is found to have had an affair with a 21-year-old White House intern, Monica Lewinsky, and then persuaded her to lie under oath about it. She is thought to be only one of many.

NATURE NOTES

Fig.1 Upright, spread-winged stance is a characteristic posture.

Kink in pecker

The Shag U.S.A.
(*Presidentia priapica*)

Its colony has hundreds, or even thousands, of birds. A vigorous breeder, it is devoted to defenceless chicks.

Peter Brookes 24 i 98

Lewinsky claims that she did have sex with Clinton in the Oval Office (dubbed the 'Oral Office'). The President denies having a sexual relationship with 'that woman'.

NATURE NOTES

Fig.1 Beavers can prove the downfall of the highest and mightiest in the land.

Eager Beaver (*Lewinskis lewdinskis*)
Is adept with huge incisors in bringing down the tallest trunks, from which it can build damming evidence.

Tony Blair warns that the West must be ready to use force against Saddam Hussein, who has the capacity to produce enough nerve gas to wipe out the world's population.

NATURE NOTES

Camel
(*Saddamus madmanus*)

Of a savage and most ill-tempered disposition, this beast is unpredictable when it gets the hump.

Fig.1 It is impossible to budge without resorting to the big stick.

Sinn Féin faces expulsion from the peace talks following two Belfast murders. The Ulster Democratic Party had already been expelled following three Catholic killings by its paramilitary associates. Northern Ireland Secretary Mo Mowlam presides.

NATURE NOTES

Spectacled Owl
(*Mowlam owlam*)

Introduced in a futile attempt to keep in check pestilential vermin. A by-word for wisdom, it can also be regarded by locals as a creature of ill-omen.

Flight pattern:

LONDON

BELFAST

The US demands that Saddam gives UN weapons inspectors access to all sites. Madeleine Albright, Secretary of State, backed by Robin Cook, threatens military action if he does not comply.

NATURE NOTE

American Eagle
(Albrighta stealthfighta)

Belligerently hawkish, the female displays unrivalled power and control in the air. Rides the desert thermals before swooping.

The young will feed on anything they are given.

21 ii 98
Peter Brookes

Lord Irvine of Lairg, Lord Chancellor, faces embarrassment over the soaring costs of refurbishing his official residence in the Palace of Westminster.

NATURE NOTES

Peacockup
(*Irvineus vainglorious*)

Indulges in a wildly extravagant display, attracting much excited attention to itself. Feathers its nest with a rich variety of exotic materials.

Fig. 1
The peacock throne

Pugin-style repeat pattern wallpaper motif

28 ii 98

Peter Brookes

The government is forced to retreat over advice given by Frank Dobson, Health Secretary, to reduce consumption of red meat following the BSE débâcle. Both Dobson and Jack Cunningham, Agriculture Secretary, have to eat their words.

Complete Bullocks *(Dobsonus cunninghamus)*

These beasts act precipitately, charging at will and jumping to the wrong conclusions. Their stock with farmers is low.

The usual suspects – including a Labour Chancellor with a Tory Budget and a Deputy Prime Minister who had suffered a drenching at the Brit Awards.

Ditto the Tories – with a Lord Archer noisily campaigning for London Mayor and a Baroness Thatcher just being noisy.

Alastair Campbell, Tony Blair's chief spin-doctor, denies accusations of lying on behalf of the Prime Minister and of bullying ministers over Budget leaks.

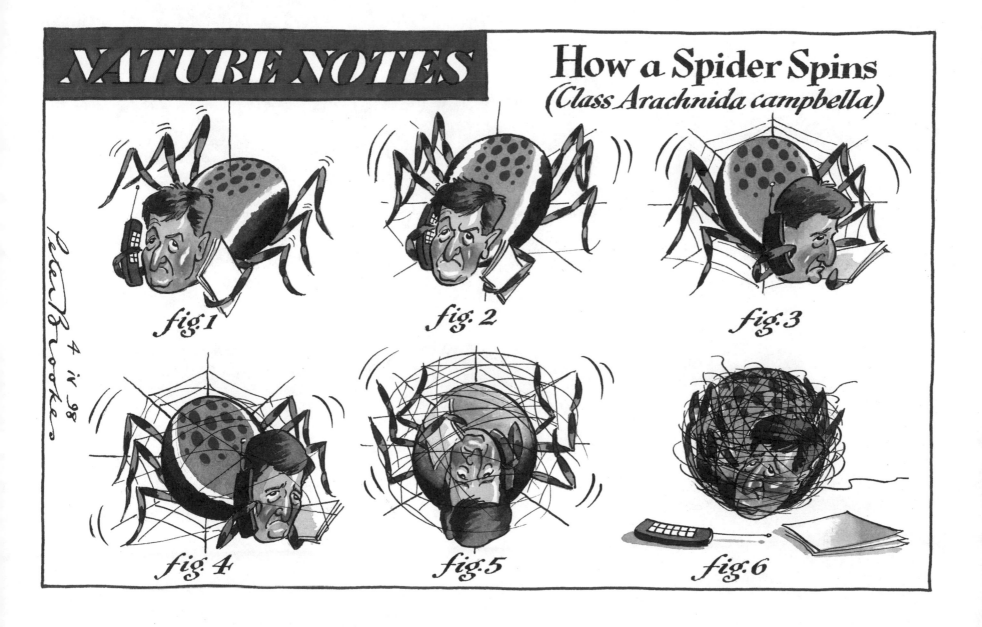

NATURE NOTES

How a Spider Spins
(Class Arachnida campbella)

fig.1

fig. 2

fig.3

fig. 4

fig.5

fig.6

Ann Widdecombe joins the shadow Cabinet, alongside Michael Howard, to take on Dobson over health. The previous year she had spectacularly ruined Howard's party leadership chances by describing him as having 'something of the night about him'.

John Prescott performs an aerial government U-turn by planning to privatise air-traffic control. He is still pursuing his 'integrated transport policy'.

Chancellor Gordon Brown announces that growth in public spending will be limited to 2.25 per cent, thereby putting pressure on 'spending' ministers. The left are also disappointed by the low level of the minimum wage.

Fig. 1

Fig. 2

Imprudent

Brown-spotted Puffedupfish *(Putanendus toboomandbustus)*
When danger threatens, the fish inflates itself into a spiky, prickly ball. Spending-hungry predators find this extremely hard to swallow. *
* *Especially when attacking from the left.*

Robin Cook is rebuked by an all-party Commons committee for refusing to allow MPs immediate access to telegrams relating to the arms-to-Africa affair.

NATURE NOTES

a. *b.* *c.*

Fig.1 Total self-absorption

Red Snapper
(Cookis irrascibilis)

Caught in Sierra Leone waters, it indulges in a disgusting and distressing act of self-destruction *(see Fig.1)*

Serving suggestion:
Try skewered and kebabbed,
thoroughly grilled, or in a stew.

27 vi 98

Peter Brookes

David Trimble, leader of the Ulster Unionists, is elected First Minister when the Northern Ireland Assembly has its inaugural meeting. The Rev. Ian Paisley and other hardline Unionists confront Sinn Féin directly in furious exchanges.

NATURE NOTES

Peter Brookes
4 vii 98

Fig.1 *Getting the pip*

Fig. 2 *Suggested sideboard arrangement*

Orange *(Citrus trimblus)*

Much sweeter than the acidic *Citrus paisleyus*, it is not Ulster's only fruit, despite its premier position. Often in a jam and full of pith.

Derek Draper, lobbyist and former chief aide to Peter Mandelson, is at the centre of a political storm over alleged cash for privileged access to Number 10. Also involved is Roger Liddle, one of Blair's leading policy advisers.

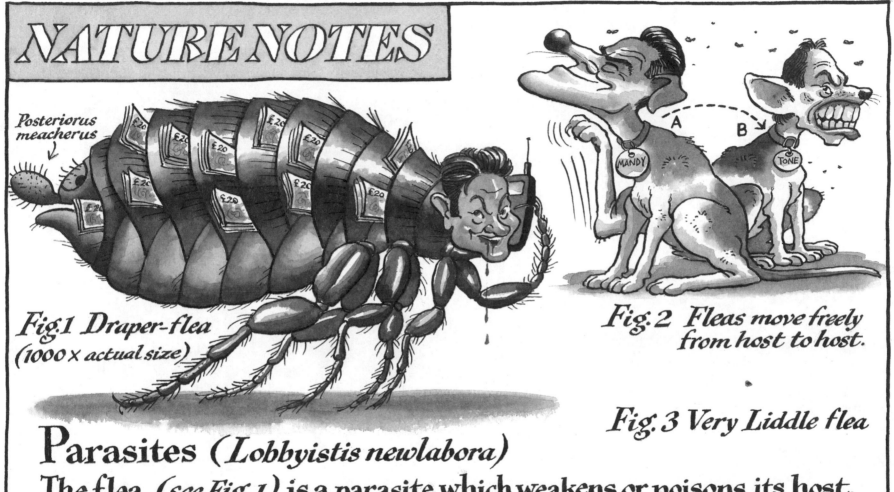

NATURE NOTES

Posteriorus meacherus

Fig. 1 Draper-flea (1000 × actual size)

Fig. 2 Fleas move freely from host to host.

Fig. 3 Very Liddle flea

Parasites (*Lobbyistis newlabora*)

The flea *(see Fig. 1)* is a parasite which weakens or poisons its host, giving nothing in return for the blood taken. It sucks.

Peter Brookes 11 vii 98

Summit meetings in Moscow between Presidents Yeltsin and Clinton are overshadowed by Russia's deepening political, economic and alcoholic crises.

NATURE NOTES

Pink Elephant
(*Yeltsinus deliriumtremens*)

Roams the steppes
and the forests of
Central Asia fuelled
by copious amounts
of high octane liquid
refreshment. Prone
to extreme, erratic
behaviour. Tsk, tsk.

Fig. 1
Jumbo recumbo

The sexually explicit Starr Report on the President's affair with Monica Lewinsky is delivered without warning to Congress, just as Clinton makes yet another apology for his behaviour to bolster ebbing Democrat support.

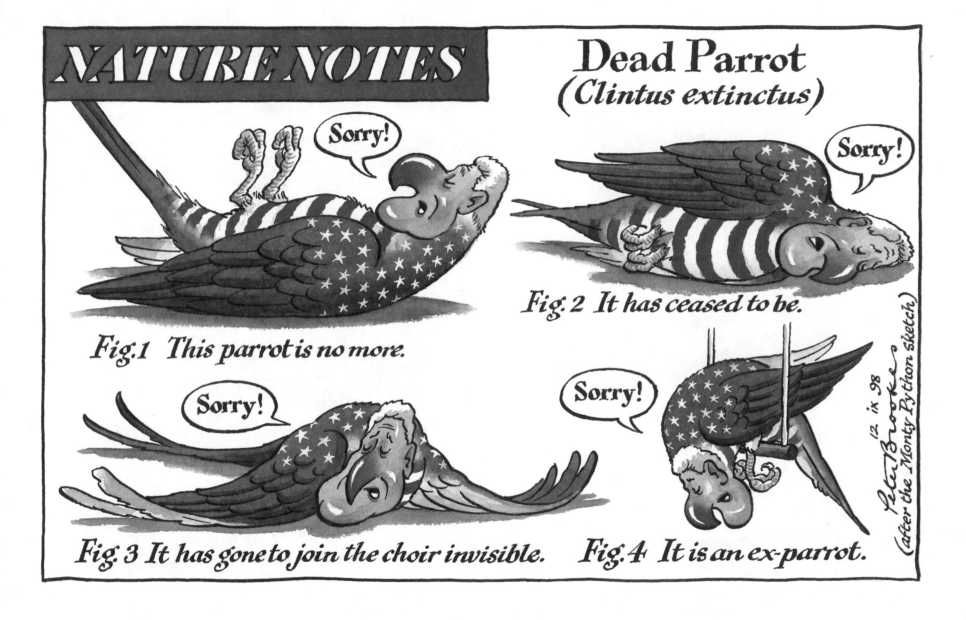

The annual conference season begins, with the Liberal Democrats at Brighton, the Tories at Bournemouth and Labour (for the last time) at Blackpool.

NATURE NOTES

Beside the Seaside

Autumn sees the familiar gathering of washed-up molluscs at our favourite coastal resorts.

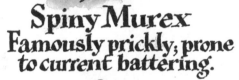

Spiny Murex
Famously prickly; prone to current battering.

Giant Razor
Remains largely hidden, the easier to wound.

Common Winkle
Generally discovered on the rocks.

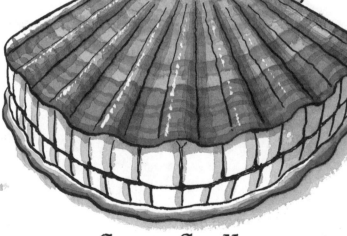

Great Scallop
All surface, with little content. Widely used as an ashtray.

Limpet
Attaches itself to others such as the Gt. Scallop (q.v.) Caught between a rock and a hard place.

19 ix 98 Peter Brookes

Victory for Social Democrat Gerhard Schröder, Germany's Tony Blair, ends the lengthy chancellorship of Helmut Kohl. It seems likely that he must govern in coalition with the Green Party.

NATURE NOTES

Peter Brookes
3 x 98

Schröderwurst

Fig.1 Sour kraut

Least Wurst (*Polonyus balonyus*)
A flavourless sausage which cannot be served on its own.
Greens, whilst horribly unpalatable, should accompany it.

An impeachment investigation along the lines of the Watergate inquiry that led to Richard Nixon's resignation is put to the vote, with some Democrats crucially siding with the majority Republicans.

Baroness Jay, Leader of the Lords, says that the government will press ahead with scrapping hereditary peers' voting rights but denies that this is an act of 'political spite or a throwback to the old battles of class war'.

NATURE NOTES

Ermine, or Stoat
(*Erminus verminus*)

More usually sighted, if at all, in a hereditary attitude of somnolent and blissful ignorance, it turns vicious when its privileged existence is threatened by the raucous Jay (*Newlabora let'sgetthebastardsa*)

Fig.1 Ermine will 'play dead' to fool predators. Sometimes they are.

Peter Brookes 17 x 98

Baroness Thatcher, who takes tea with General Augusto Pinochet, calls for the immediate release of the former Chilean dictator, who is under arrest in a London clinic following an extradition request from Spain on charges of murder and human rights abuses.

NATURE NOTES

Chilean Llama
(*Nevertrustus augustus*)

This *bête-noir* fights viciously for supremacy of the flock. Attempts by the domesticated form to acclimatise itself in England have proved disastrous. Seeks the high ground.

Fig. 1 Llamas like nothing better than a nice English cuppa.

In this Style 10/6

Welsh Secretary Ron Davies resigns from the Cabinet in bizarre circumstances over a 'serious lapse of judgement' arising from a visit to Clapham Common, a known gay meeting-place. He claims to have been robbed at knifepoint.

William Hague's leadership of the Conservative Party is in crisis after he is forced to sack Lord Cranborne, Tory leader in the House of Lords, and the remainder of the Tory front bench offer to resign. Cranborne had unilaterally done a deal with the government over Lords reform which Hague publicly rejected.

NATURE NOTES

Partridge in a Peer Tree
(Delicious withcranbornejellyus)

Seasonal game much fancied carved-up at the tables of superannuated and over-privileged lords-a-leaping.

Fig.1 Give it a jolly good basting. Serve thoroughly roasted & well stuffed.

The trial of Bill Clinton, for perjury and bringing the office of the presidency into disrepute, opens.

NATURE NOTES

Albatross
(Monica givesgoodfellatio)

A gigantic, deep-throated bird of ill-omen with very interesting feeding habits (gorges on flies). It can keep going for hours at a time, heading south. Sails dangerously close to the wind.

Fig.1
Egg

Questioned over his increasing links with the Liberal Democrats, Tony Blair dismisses the idea that he is planning to give Paddy Ashdown a Cabinet job.

NATURE NOTES

Fig. 1

CHOMP

Brown-nosed Plover (*Neversmilus atacrocodilus*)

Keeps clean the orifices of *crocodilidae*. Feeds off host by picking its teeth for scraps. Gets its just desserts. (*see Fig.1*)

16 i 99

Peter Brookes

William Hague, in a speech to the right-wing Centre for Policy Studies, promises to remould the Conservatives as a modern, forward-looking alternative to New Labour. It would avoid harking back to warm beer and friendly vicars and would embrace 'the bold, the brassy, the vigorous, the exciting'. This was 'The British Way', Hague's answer to Blair's 'Third Way'.

NATURE NOTES

Brassyca
(*Brassica crassica*)

Tasteless and prematurely running to seed, this vegetable desperately seeks a place in The Sun. The northern-rooted cabbage totally fails to excite the discerning palate, however imaginatively it is presented (*see Fig. 1*).

Fig. 1

The Prince of Wales and Camilla Parker Bowles finally, if reluctantly, confirm what has long been common knowledge when they very publicly leave a party at the Ritz Hotel together.

NATURE NOTES

Potted   Potty

Avoid planting near snapdragons

Fig.1

Camellia *(Paramour carolus)*

This old favourite wilts in the glare of The Sun, preferring the shade, but can adapt eventually to a more exposed position with careful nurturing.

Peter Brookes 30 i 99

Glenn Hoddle is sacked as England's football coach after his suggestion in an interview with *The Times* that disabled people were paying for the sins of a previous life. Even the Prime Minister gets involved, which seals Hoddle's fate.

Ministers are shaken by the media and public outcry over the safety (or otherwise) of genetically modified food and by claims that the government is too close to the industry. They are, of course, themselves genetically modified.

NATURE NOTES

GM Tomato (*Theapplianceus ofscienceus*)

Synthetically adapted for maximum consumption and lasting palatability. Long term health fears are growing.

Fig.1 Original crop

Fig.2 Genetically modified

Sir Paul Condon, the Metropolitan Police Commissioner, refuses to resign over the report into the murder of Stephen Lawrence, which concludes that there was 'pernicious and institutionalised racism' in the Metropolitan Police.

NATURE NOTES

Bluebottle
(Defectivus detectivus)

Attracted to bad meat, it sits atop the festering rubbish tip in the Yard (*see Fig.1*). This pernicious pest avoids all efforts to get it to buzz off (*see Fig.2*).

Fig.1

Fig.2

Bluebottle's 'Not me, Guv' configuration

Peter Brookes 27 ii 99

Chancellor Gordon Brown's tax-cutting Budget package is not a blessing to everyone.

NATURE NOTES | How to Hold a Budgetigar

If you are a childless, married, self-employed mortgagor who smokes, and drives a normal-sized car, you might wish to adopt the recommended hand position thus:

X WRONG

✔ RIGHT

13 iii 99
Peter Brookes

Nato is ordered to begin air-strikes against the former Yugoslavia after Slobodan Milosevic rejects last-minute diplomatic efforts over Kosovo; the Law Lords rule that General Pinochet has no immunity from prosecution for alleged crimes committed after 1988; and IRA prisoners serving life sentences for bomb plots in England are released early from the Maze prison.

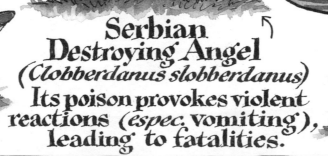

NATURE NOTES
Toxic Mushrooms

Chilean Sickener
(Wewon'tmissimo generalissimo)
**Induces a chronic head-
ache with gut-wrenching,
stomach-churning
nausea.**

↓

↱ *Grows on old dung
and Straw*

Serbian
Destroying Angel
(Clobberdanus slobberdanus)
**Its poison provokes violent
reactions (espec. vomiting),
leading to fatalities.**

Irish
Death Hood
*(Earlyreleaseus
threatensthepeaceus)*
**Causes the gorge to rise and
excruciating pain in kneecaps.**

↓

27 iii 99

Peter Brookes

After marathon negotiations at Hillsborough Castle, Tony Blair and Bertie Ahern publish their joint plan for implementing the Good Friday peace accord, then send the parties away for a twelve-day 'pause for reflection', but crucially fail to break the deadlock over IRA disarmament.

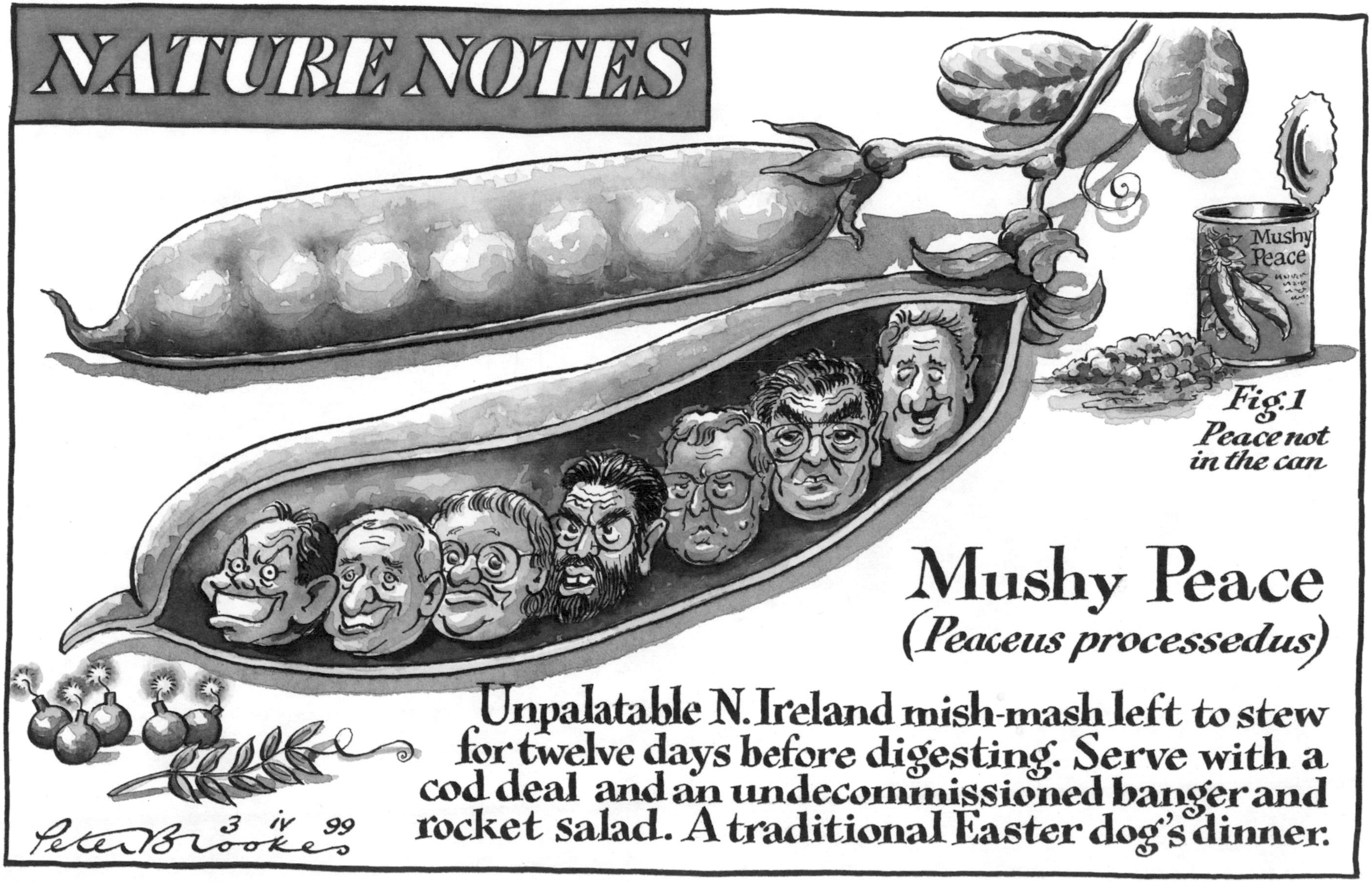
NATURE NOTES
Mushy Peace
Fig.1
Peace not in the can
Mushy Peace
(Peaceus processedus)
Unpalatable N. Ireland mish-mash left to stew for twelve days before digesting. Serve with a cod deal and an undecommissioned banger and rocket salad. A traditional Easter dog's dinner.
Peter Brookes 3 iv 99

Defence Secretary George Robertson and Foreign Secretary Robin Cook attempt to justify the continuing Nato bombing of Yugoslavia at daily briefings, to contrasting effect.

NATURE NOTES

Nato Potato
(*Newlaboris bellicosis*)

A late-maturing, thick-skinned variety with a high starch content which is nevertheless proving a popular staple of the wartime austerity menu. Try with Spam.

Tubers

10 iv 99

Peter Brookes

Fig. 1
Flak-jacket potato

ROBERTSON

Fig. 2
Spud-u-don't-like

Tory strategists launch (yet another) campaign to revamp William Hague's image as a down-to-earth man of the people in the run-up to May's local elections. In the event, the Tories recover some ground and consolidate still further in the European elections a few weeks later, thereby giving Blair his first real taste of failure.

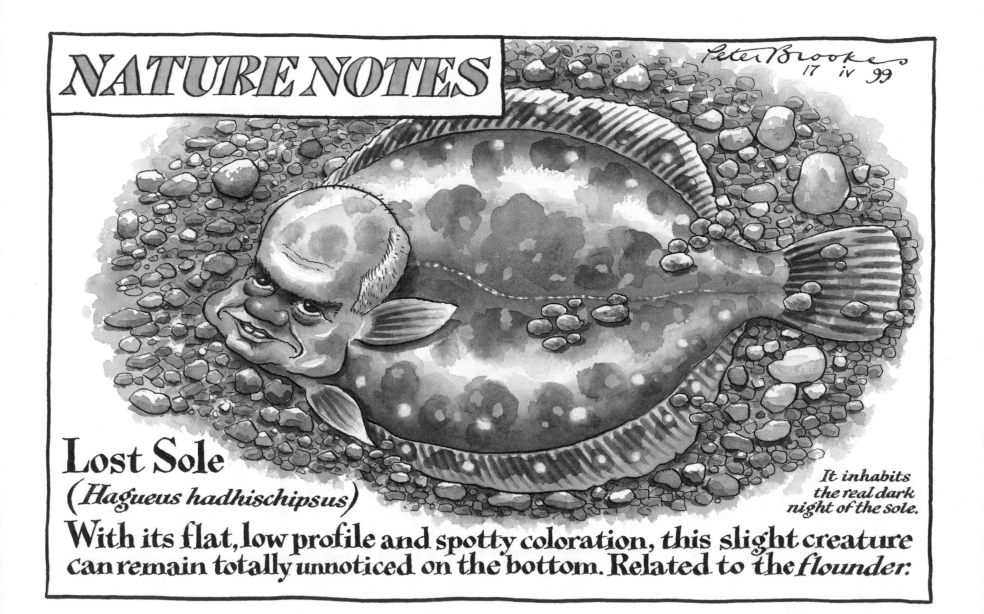

NATURE NOTES

Lost Sole
(*Hagueus hadhischipsus*)

With its flat, low profile and spotty coloration, this slight creature can remain totally unnoticed on the bottom. Related to the *flounder*.

It inhabits the real dark night of the sole.

Nato bombs miss their targets in Kosovo and Serbia, claiming many innocent lives. Meanwhile Tony Blair takes a message of hawkish resolve to America, where distinctly wobbly Nato heads are holding an anniversary summit.

NATURE NOTES

Peter Brookes 1 v 99

Men-o'-war
(Bellicosis jellycosis)

Colonial organisms which are full of gas and drift with the winds and tides of public opinion. They deliver a vicious sting which often misses the target.

Fig. 1 Not to be confused with the totally harmless & innocuous common jellyfish.

New Labour scores a historic election victory, creating the first Scottish parliament for three hundred years. But it is denied an overall majority and must form a coalition for the first time since the Second World War. Donald Dewar is set to become Scotland's First Minister.

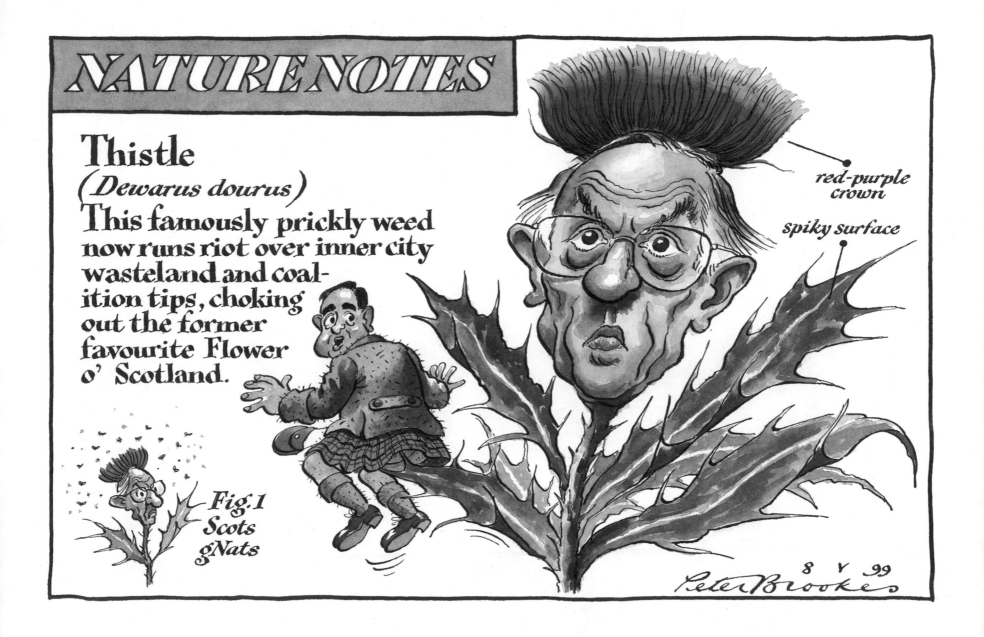

Lawrence Dallaglio, of Wasps and England, steps down as England's rugby union captain after allegations in the *News of the World* that he had been a drug-dealer and had taken cocaine and Ecstasy during a Lions tour. He believes he was set up in an interview with two journalists, one of whom was a young 'buxom blonde'.

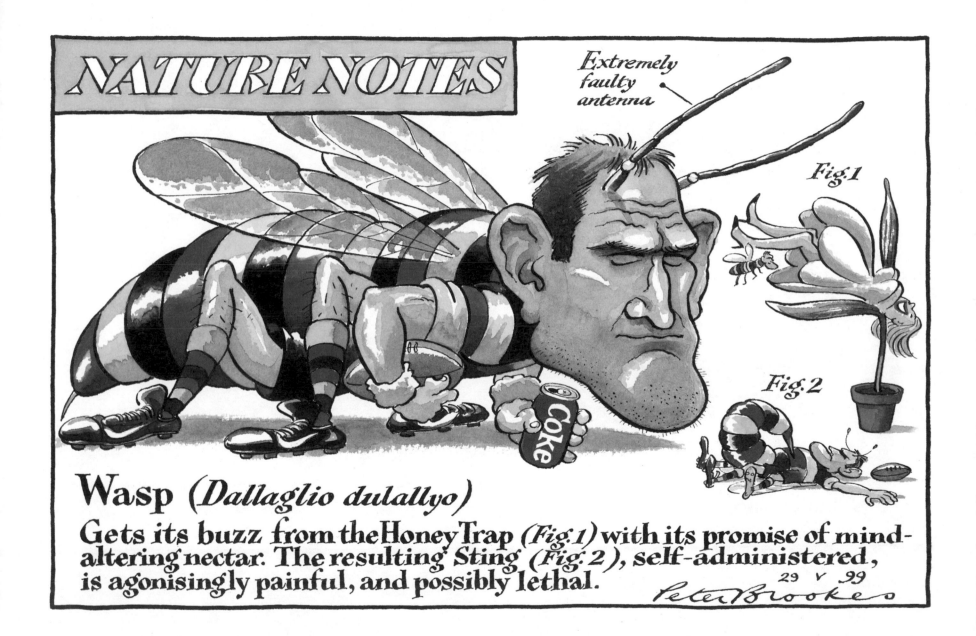

Jonathan Aitken, who famously resigned as Chief Secretary to the Treasury to fight a libel action against the *Guardian* newspaper and Granada Television – 'with the simple sword of truth and the trusty shield of British fair play' – gets eighteen months for perjury and starts his sentence at Belmarsh prison.

NATURE NOTES

Jailbird
(*Aitkenus inchokeyus*)

High-flier which can take a dive at breakneck speed. Captured on the inhospitable Belmarshes where it ekes out a miserable existence on porridge.

Fig.1 Jailbirds are tasty barbecued. Just skewer on a simple sword of truth and roast for eighteen months (or seven with remission). Serve on a trusty shield of British fair play.

12 vi 99

Peter Brookes